Billy and Tom went to play in the mud.

Billy slid in the mud.

Slip, slop, splat!

Tom slid in the mud.

Slip, slop, splat!

Billy was flat in the mud.

He was stuck.

Tom was flat in the mud.

He was stuck.

Dad went to look for Billy
and Tom.
Slip, slop, splat!
Dad was flat in the mud too.

Billy had a plan.

He got on his dad's back.

He slid along his back.

Then he went flop, plop
and he fell on the grass.

Tom got on his dad's back.
He slid along his back.
Then he went flop, plop on
to the grass.

Billy and Tom went to pull dad out of the mud.

Pull ... pull ... pull ... Yes!

Dad slid out of the mud.